THE Jesse Tree
ADVENT JOURNAL

DISCIPLE of CHRIST
EDUCATION IN VIRTUE

Copyright © 2019 Education in Virtue. All rights reserved. No part of this publication may be reproduced or transmitted in any form or means, electronic or mechanical, including photocopy, recording, or information storage and retrieval system, without the permission in writing from the publisher.

Published by Lumen Ecclesiae Press
4101 East Joy Road
Ann Arbor, Michigan 48105

Scripture texts in this work are taken from the New American Bible, revised edition © 2010, 1991, 1986, 1970 Confraternity of Christian Doctrine, Washington, D.C. and are used by permission of the copyright owner. All rights reserved. No part of the New American Bible may be reproduced in any form without permission in writing from the copyright owner.

General Editor: Sister Teresa Benedicta Block
Editor: Sister John Dominic Rasmussen, O.P.
Cover and Book Design: Rachel Salazar
Book Layout and Permissions: Linda Kelly
Copy Editor: Claudia Volkman
Contributions: Sally Wagner

ISBN 978-1-7323200-7-9

First Printing
Printed in the United States of America

Requests for permission to make copies of any part of the work should be directed to: educationinvirtue.com

Table of Contents

Introduction 5
My Reading Schedule 6
Advent Virtues 8
Advent Symbols 9
Lectio Divina 10
Daily Readings 12
Credits 108

But a shoot shall sprout from the stump of Jesse,
and from his roots a bud shall blossom.
The spirit of the LORD shall rest upon him:
a spirit of wisdom and of understanding,
A spirit of counsel and of strength,
a spirit of knowledge and of fear of the LORD,
and his delight shall be the fear of the LORD.
Not by appearance shall he judge,
nor by hearsay shall he decide,
But he shall judge the poor with justice,
and decide fairly for the land's afflicted.
He shall strike the ruthless with the rod of his mouth,
and with the breath of his lips he shall slay the wicked.

Isaiah 11:1-4

Introduction

Whenever my grandparents visited, we would ask them to tell us about the past. We wanted to know what it was like when they were little, we wanted to hear family stories, and we wanted to know more about the people in the black and white photographs. Those stories from long ago were part of our history and helped us to see how our family came to be.

In Advent, we prepare for the coming of the Messiah. We look forward to Christ's second coming, and we look back to that moment in time when Christ was born in Bethlehem. What was His human history? What were the family stories of Jesus? Who were His ancestors? Since the beginning of the Church, Christians have been telling one another about the stories and events which preceded the coming of Christ.

There is a beautiful prophesy in Scripture about a branch or shoot coming from the stump of Jesse. A tree stump looks dead, but a new branch from that stump can grow into something marvelous. This living shoot coming from a seemingly dead tree is an image of Christ. Unlike His ancestors who died, the tree which is Jesus is eternal. Christ conquers death and brings us lasting joy.

Although Jesus is the Way, the Truth, and the Life, His human history is still important. We understand Christ and ourselves better when we understand the past. For this reason, starting in the Middle Ages, it became a tradition to share the family stories of Jesus when preparing for Christmas. Christians made paper ornaments of the people and events who came before Christ. During the days leading up to Christmas, these ornaments were displayed on a tree. This practice became known as making a "Jesse Tree" and is still done in many homes today.

This Advent journal is a reflection on the Jesse Tree. It follows the people who came before Jesus and longed for His coming. May their stories teach us to open wide our hearts to the presence of Christ, God with us.

My Reading Schedule

Traditionally the stories of Christ's family history are reflected upon during the twenty-five days leading up to Christmas. Ideally, one would start the journal on December 1 and complete it on December 25. However, given work and school schedules, you may want to start the journal sooner. Use the chart on the next page to fill in the dates that you would like to use the journal so that it can be completed in time for the celebration of Jesus' birth.

Day 1	
Day 2	
Day 3	
Day 4	
Day 5	
Day 6	
Day 7	
Day 8	
Day 9	
Day 10	
Day 11	
Day 12	
Day 13	

Day 14	
Day 15	
Day 16	
Day 17	
Day 18	
Day 19	
Day 20	
Day 21	
Day 22	
Day 23	
Day 24	
Day 25	

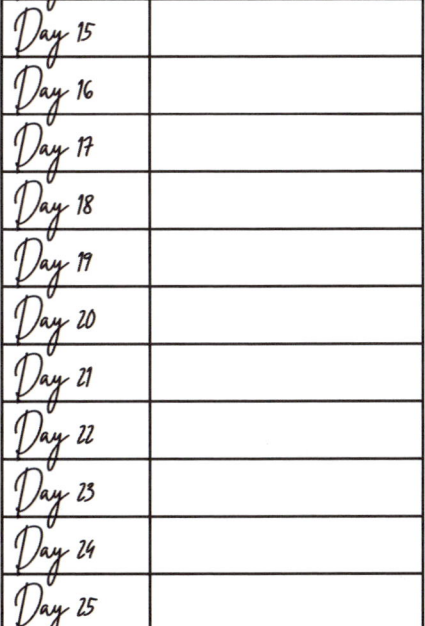

Advent Virtues

Virtue	Knowing the Virtue	Living the Virtue	Scripture Connection
Prayerfulness	Being still, listening, and being willing to talk to God as a friend	• Making personal visits to the Blessed Sacrament • Taking initiative to pray • Practicing recollection	"Mary kept all these things, reflecting on them in her heart." *(Luke 2:19)*
Humility	Awareness that all our gifts come from God and appreciation of the gifts of others	• Acknowledging the talents of others by praising them • Saying "thank you" when praised for an action well done	"And Mary said, 'My soul proclaims the greatness of the Lord.'" *(Luke 1:46)*
Obedience	Assenting to rightful authority without hesitation or resistance	• Honoring your teachers and parents by doing what they ask • Anticipating their requests and wants • Smiling while doing a task you should do	"When Joseph awoke, he did as the angel of the Lord had commanded him and took his wife into his home." *(Matthew 1:24)*
Generosity	Giving of oneself in a willing and cheerful manner for the good of others	• Willingly helping others • Freely giving of your time and gifts	"For God so loved the world that he gave his only Son…" *(John 3:16)*
Gratitude	Thankful disposition of mind and heart	• Expressing thanks by words or deeds and in your prayers	"The Mighty One has done great things for me, and holy is his name." *(Luke 1:49)*
Patience	Bearing present difficulties calmly	• Waiting for your turn • Listening while others are speaking • Remaining calm when you don't get what you want	"…And Joseph too went up from Galilee from the town of Nazareth to Judea, to the city of David that is called Bethlehem…" *(Luke 2:4)*
Docility	Willingness to be taught	• Willingness to listen to directions • Listening to and thinking about another person's idea	"When the angels went away to heaven, the shepherds said to one another, 'Let us go, then, to Bethlehem…'" *(Luke 2:15)*

Advent Symbols

Date	Event/Person	Scripture	Symbol
Dec. 1	Adam and Eve	Genesis 3:1–24	Apple
Dec. 2	Noah and the flood	Genesis 6, 7, 8:1–9	Ark
Dec. 3	God's promise to Noah	Genesis 9:8–17	Rainbow
Dec. 4	God's covenant with Abraham	Genesis 12:1–3; 18:1–5	Stars (representing his descendants)
Dec. 5	Abraham's sacrifice	Genesis 22:1–18	Ram and altar
Dec. 6	Jacob's dream	Genesis 28:10–22	Ladder
Dec. 7	Joseph saves Israel	Exodus 2:23–4:20	Coat of many colors
Dec. 8	God calls Moses	Exodus 2:23–4:20	Burning bush
Dec. 9	God feeds His people	Exodus 16:1–36	Manna and quail
Dec. 10	God gives Moses His laws	Exodus 19–20:1–2	Stone tablets
Dec. 11	Wall of Jericho falls	Joshua 6:1–20	Horns
Dec. 12	Ruth helps Naomi	Ruth 1–4	Bushel of wheat
Dec. 13	God calls Samuel	1 Samuel 3:1–21	Boy sleeping
Dec. 14	Jesse's family is chosen	1 Samuel 16:1–13 (Isaiah 11:1)	Branch growing from stump
Dec. 15	David kills Goliath	1 Samuel 17:1–54	Sling and stone
Dec. 16	Solomon's wisdom	1 Kings 3:3–28	Light (torch)
Dec. 17	God takes Elijah to heaven	2 Kings 2:1–13	Chariot of fire
Dec. 18	Daniel in the lion's den	Daniel 6:1–28	Lion
Dec. 19	Jonah in the whale	Jonah 1 and 2	Whale
Dec. 20	The Blessed Virgin Mary	Matthew 1:23 and Isaiah 7:14	White Rose
Dec. 21	Gabriel appears to Mary	Luke 1:26–38	Angel
Dec. 22	St. Joseph	Matthew 1:18–25	Carpenter's tool
Dec. 23	Mary and Joseph travel to Bethlehem	Luke 2:1–5	Mary and Joseph on donkey
Dec. 24	Wise Men follow the star	Matthew 2:1–12	Star

Lectio Divina

Jesus Christ said, "Learn from me" (Matthew 11:29) and offered his life as a model for us. To be a disciple of Christ means we seek to learn from Him on how to live as His disciple. Through reading and meditating on the Word of God, we come to know Him and develop a personal relationship with Him.

Reading (Lectio)
What does the Word of God say?
Read slowly, listening attentively to the Word of God.

Meditation (Meditatio)
What does the Word of God say to me?
Spend time with the word or phrase that touched your heart.

Prayer (Oratio)
What do I say to the Lord in response to His Word?
Let the word or phrase shape your response to God, such as praise, petition, thanksgiving.

Contemplation (Contemplatio)
What conversion of mind, heart, and life is the Lord asking of me?
Rest in His presence, and open your heart to receive His Love.

Action (Actio)
How has encountering God's love in His Word changed me?
How can my life be a gift to others?
Ask the Lord to show you where to grow in virtue.

"I would like in particular to recall and recommend the ancient tradition of *Lectio Divina*: the diligent reading of Sacred Scripture accompanied by prayer brings about that intimate dialogue in which the person reading hears God who is speaking, and in praying, responds to him with trusting openness of heart (cf. *Dei Verbum,* n.25) If it is effectively promoted, this practice will bring to the Church—I am convinced of it—a new spiritual springtime."

— **Pope Benedict XVI**

day 1 Genesis 3:1-24

Adam and Eve

Now the snake was the most cunning of all the wild animals that the LORD God had made. He asked the woman, "Did God really say, 'You shall not eat from any of the trees in the garden'?" The woman answered the snake: "We may eat of the fruit of the trees in the garden; it is only about the fruit of the tree in the middle of the garden that God said, 'You shall not eat it or even touch it, or else you will die.'" But the snake said to the woman: "You certainly will not die! God knows well that when you eat of it your eyes will be opened and you will be like gods, who know good and evil." The woman saw that the tree was good for food and pleasing to the eyes, and the tree was desirable for gaining wisdom. So she took some of its fruit and ate it; and she also gave some to her husband, who was with her, and he ate it. Then the eyes of both of them were opened, and they knew that they were naked; so they sewed fig leaves together and made loincloths for themselves.

When they heard the sound of the LORD God walking about in the garden at the breezy time of the day, the man and his wife hid themselves from the LORD God among the trees of the garden. The LORD God then called to the man and asked him: Where are you? He answered, "I heard you in the garden; but I was afraid, because I was naked, so I hid." Then God asked: Who told you that you were naked? Have you eaten from the tree of which I had forbidden you to eat? The man replied, "The woman whom you put here with me—she gave me fruit from the tree, so I ate it." The LORD God then asked the woman: What is this you have done? The woman answered, "The snake tricked me, so I ate it."

Then the LORD God said to the snake:

Because you have done this,
  cursed are you
  among all the animals, tame or wild;
On your belly you shall crawl,
  and dust you shall eat
  all the days of your life.

I will put enmity between you and the woman,
  and between your offspring and hers;
They will strike at your head,
  while you strike at their heel.

To the woman he said:

I will intensify your toil in childbearing;
  in pain you shall bring forth children.
Yet your urge shall be for your husband,
  and he shall rule over you.

To the man he said: Because you listened to your wife and ate from the tree about which I commanded you, You shall not eat from it,

Cursed is the ground because of you!
  In toil you shall eat its yield
  all the days of your life.
Thorns and thistles it shall bear for you,
  and you shall eat the grass of the field.
By the sweat of your brow
  you shall eat bread,
Until you return to the ground,
  from which you were taken;
For you are dust,
  and to dust you shall return.

The man gave his wife the name "Eve," because she was the mother of all the living.

The LORD God made for the man and his wife garments of skin, with which he clothed them. Then the LORD God said: See! The man has become like one of us, knowing good and evil! Now, what if he also reaches out his hand to take fruit from the tree of life, and eats of it and lives forever? The LORD God therefore banished him from the garden of Eden, to till the ground from which he had been taken. He expelled the man, stationing the cherubim and the fiery revolving sword east of the garden of Eden, to guard the way to the tree of life.

God's word strikes the heart. What word or phrase touched your heart?

In the Garden, Eve chose her own way instead of listening to God. Adam chose to do nothing when he should have been guarding the garden and protecting his wife. Which fault do you struggle with more—choosing your own way or not standing up for what is right? How might a greater trust in God help? Write your own meditation or prayer below.

Use this space to sketch or doodle the symbol for the Scripture—APPLE

What are some ways you can strengthen yourself to resist temptation?

_____
_____
_____

Write a prayer asking God for strength and help when tempted.

_____
_____
_____
_____
_____
_____

day 2   Genesis 7:6–23

Noah and the Flood

Noah was six hundred years old when the flood came upon the earth. Together with his sons, his wife, and his sons' wives, Noah went into the ark because of the waters of the flood. Of the clean animals and the unclean, of the birds, and of everything that crawls on the ground, two by two, male and female came to Noah into the ark, just as God had commanded him. When the seven days were over, the waters of the flood came upon the earth.

In the six hundredth year of Noah's life, in the second month, on the seventeenth day of the month: on that day

All the fountains of the great abyss burst forth,
  and the floodgates of the sky were opened.

For forty days and forty nights heavy rain poured down on the earth.

On the very same day, Noah and his sons Shem, Ham, and Japheth, and Noah's wife, and the three wives of Noah's sons had entered the ark, together with every kind of wild animal, every kind of tame animal, every kind of crawling thing that crawls on the earth, and every kind of bird. Pairs of all creatures in which there was the breath of life came to Noah into the ark. Those that entered were male and female; of all creatures they came, as God had commanded Noah. Then the LORD shut him in.

The flood continued upon the earth for forty days. As the waters increased, they lifted the ark, so that it rose above the earth. The waters swelled and increased greatly on the earth, but the ark floated on the surface of the waters. Higher and higher on the earth the waters swelled, until all the highest mountains under the heavens were submerged. The waters swelled fifteen cubits higher than the submerged mountains. All creatures that moved on earth perished: birds, tame animals, wild animals, and all that teemed on the earth, as well as all humankind. Everything on dry land with the breath of life in its nostrils died. The LORD wiped out every being on earth: human beings and animals, the crawling things and the birds of the air; all were wiped out from the earth. Only Noah and those with him in the ark were left.

God's word strikes the heart. What word or phrase touched your heart?

_____

_____

_____

In Noah's time, humanity distanced itself from God by sin. To cleanse the earth, God permitted the flood to occur. Why is it a good thing that sin often results in bad consequences?

_____

_____

_____

Use this space to sketch or doodle the symbol for the Scripture—ARK

By telling Noah to build an ark and save his family as well as the animals, God showed the depths of his love and mercy. The ark is often said to represent the Church. How does the Church shelter and keep us safe?

_____

_____

_____

Write a prayer expressing your sorrow for any sin that has distanced you from God or other people.

_____
_____
_____
_____
_____

day 3 — Genesis 9:1-17

God's Promise to Noah

God blessed Noah and his sons and said to them: Be fertile and multiply and fill the earth. Fear and dread of you shall come upon all the animals of the earth and all the birds of the air, upon all the creatures that move about on the ground and all the fishes of the sea; into your power they are delivered. Any living creature that moves about shall be yours to eat; I give them all to you as I did the green plants. Only meat with its lifeblood still in it you shall not eat. Indeed for your own lifeblood I will demand an accounting: from every animal I will demand it, and from a human being, each one for the blood of another, I will demand an accounting for human life.

Anyone who sheds the blood
   of a human being,
 by a human being shall that one's
   blood be shed;
For in the image of God
  have human beings been made.

Be fertile, then, and multiply; abound on earth and subdue it.

God said to Noah and to his sons with him: See, I am now establishing my covenant with you and your descendants after you and with every living creature that was with you: the birds, the tame animals, and all the wild animals that were with you—all that came out of the ark. I will establish my covenant with you, that never again shall all creatures be destroyed by the waters of a flood; there shall not be another flood to devastate the earth. God said: This is the sign of the covenant that I am making between me and you and every living creature with you for all ages to come: I set my bow in the clouds to serve as a sign of the covenant between me and the earth. When I bring clouds over the earth, and the bow appears in the clouds, I will remember my covenant between me and you and every living creature—every mortal being—so that the waters will never again become a flood to destroy every mortal being. When the bow appears in the clouds, I will see it and remember the everlasting covenant between God and every living creature—every mortal being that is on earth. God told Noah: This is the sign of the covenant I have established between me and every mortal being that is on earth.

" I set my bow in the clouds to serve as a sign

of the covenant between me and the earth."

Genesis 9:13

God's word strikes the heart. What word or phrase touched your heart?

_____

_____

_____

After Noah prays and offers a sacrifice, God promises to always show mercy to human beings. This is God's covenant with Noah. A covenant is an official promise that establishes a relationship. What does God promise specifically and what is the sign or reminder of this covenant?

_____

_____

_____

_____

Use this space to sketch or doodle the symbol for the Scripture—RAINBOW

What signs do you have to help you remember how much God cares for and loves you?

_____

_____

Write a prayer thanking God for the covenant He made with you at your baptism which made you a part of the family of God.

_____
_____
_____
_____
_____
_____

day 4   *Genesis 12:1-3; 18:1-5*

God's Covenant with Abraham

The LORD said to Abram: Go forth from your land, your relatives, and from your father's house to a land that I will show you. I will make of you a great nation, and I will bless you; I will make your name great, so that you will be a blessing. I will bless those who bless you and curse those who curse you. All the families of the earth will find blessing in you. —*Genesis 12:1–3*

The LORD appeared to Abraham by the oak of Mamre, as he sat in the entrance of his tent, while the day was growing hot. Looking up, he saw three men standing near him. When he saw them, he ran from the entrance of the tent to greet them; and bowing to the ground, he said: "Sir, if it please you, do not go on past your servant. Let some water be brought, that you may bathe your feet, and then rest under the tree. Now that you have come to your servant, let me bring you a little food, that you may refresh yourselves; and afterward you may go on your way." "Very well," they replied, "do as you have said." —*Genesis 18:1-5*

When he saw them, he ran from the entrance of the tent

to greet them; and bowing to the ground, he said:

"Sir, if it please you, do not go on past your servant.

Genesis 18:2–3

God's word strikes the heart. What word or phrase touched your heart?

_____
_____
_____

What is God's covenant with Abraham? How is it different than the covenant with Noah?

_____
_____
_____
_____

Use this space to sketch or doodle the symbol for the Scripture—STARS

How can you be a blessing for others?

_____
_____
_____

Write a prayer reflecting on some of the ways God has blessed you.

_____
_____
_____
_____
_____
_____

day 5   Genesis 22:1-18

Abraham's Sacrifice

Some time afterward, God put Abraham to the test and said to him: Abraham! "Here I am!" he replied. Then God said: Take your son Isaac, your only one, whom you love, and go to the land of Moriah. There offer him up as a burnt offering on one of the heights that I will point out to you. Early the next morning Abraham saddled his donkey, took with him two of his servants and his son Isaac, and after cutting the wood for the burnt offering, set out for the place of which God had told him.

On the third day Abraham caught sight of the place from a distance. Abraham said to his servants: "Stay here with the donkey, while the boy and I go on over there. We will worship and then come back to you." So Abraham took the wood for the burnt offering and laid it on his son Isaac, while he himself carried the fire and the knife. As the two walked on together, Isaac spoke to his father Abraham. "Father!" he said. "Here I am," he replied. Isaac continued, "Here are the fire and the wood, but where is the sheep for the burnt offering?" "My son," Abraham answered, "God will provide the sheep for the burnt offering." Then the two walked on together.

When they came to the place of which God had told him, Abraham built an altar there and arranged the wood on it. Next he bound his son Isaac, and put him on top of the wood on the altar. Then Abraham reached out and took the knife to slaughter his son. But the angel of the LORD called to him from heaven, "Abraham, Abraham!" "Here I am," he answered. "Do not lay your hand on the boy," said the angel. "Do not do the least thing to him. For now I know that you fear God, since you did not withhold from me your son, your only one." Abraham looked up and saw a single ram caught by its horns in the thicket. So Abraham went and took the ram and offered it up as a burnt offering in place of his son. Abraham named that place Yahweh-yireh; hence people today say, "On the mountain the LORD will provide."

A second time the angel of the LORD called to Abraham from heaven and said: "I swear by my very self—oracle of the LORD—that because you acted as you did in not withholding from me your son, your only one, I will bless you and make your descendants as countless as the stars of the sky and the sands of the seashore; your descendants will take possession of the gates of their enemies, and in your descendants all the nations of the earth will find blessing, because you obeyed my command."

" I will bless you and make your descendants as countless as the stars of the sky and the sands of the seashore; your descendants will take possession of the gates of their enemies.

Genesis 22:17

God's word strikes the heart. What word or phrase touched your heart?

_____
_____
_____

God blesses Abraham abundantly, but in return, God expects Abraham to be willing to give Him everything. Why does God want us to give Him all of our heart with nothing held back?

_____
_____
_____
_____

Use this space to sketch or doodle the symbol for the Scripture—RAM and ALTAR

What are some ways God has provided for you?

_____
_____
_____

In prayer, ask God to show you where you hold back and where you need to make more room for Him. Write down what He says to you.

_____
_____
_____
_____
_____
_____

day 6 *Genesis 28:10-22*

Jacob's Dream

Jacob departed from Beer-sheba and proceeded toward Haran. When he came upon a certain place, he stopped there for the night, since the sun had already set. Taking one of the stones at the place, he put it under his head and lay down in that place. Then he had a dream: a stairway rested on the ground, with its top reaching to the heavens; and God's angels were going up and down on it. And there was the LORD standing beside him and saying: I am the LORD, the God of Abraham your father and the God of Isaac; the land on which you are lying I will give to you and your descendants. Your descendants will be like the dust of the earth, and through them you will spread to the west and the east, to the north and the south. In you and your descendants all the families of the earth will find blessing. I am with you and will protect you wherever you go, and bring you back to this land. I will never leave you until I have done what I promised you.

When Jacob awoke from his sleep, he said, "Truly, the LORD is in this place and I did not know it!" He was afraid and said: "How awesome this place is! This is nothing else but the house of God, the gateway to heaven!" Early the next morning Jacob took the stone that he had put under his head, set it up as a sacred pillar, and poured oil on top of it. He named that place Bethel, whereas the former name of the town had been Luz.

Jacob then made this vow: "If God will be with me and protect me on this journey I am making and give me food to eat and clothes to wear, and I come back safely to my father's house, the LORD will be my God. This stone that I have set up as a sacred pillar will be the house of God. Of everything you give me, I will return a tenth part to you without fail."

"How awesome this place is! This is nothing else but

the house of God, the gateway to heaven!"

Genesis 28:17

God's word strikes the heart. What word or phrase touched your heart?

_____
_____
_____

What do you think it means that there is a stairway from earth to Heaven with angels going up and down it?

_____
_____
_____

Use this space to sketch or doodle the symbol for the Scripture—LADDER

Jacob sets up a stone to remind him of how good God is to him and that God cares. When is a time you experienced God's love? How did God make His presence known to you?

_____
_____
_____

Consider how close God is to you and how His angels are all around you. Write down how God's love and presence makes you feel.

___

___

___

___

___

___

day 7 Genesis 37:2-28, 45:3-8

Joseph Saves Israel

This is the story of the family of Jacob. When Joseph was seventeen years old, he was tending the flocks with his brothers; he was an assistant to the sons of his father's wives Bilhah and Zilpah, and Joseph brought their father bad reports about them. Israel loved Joseph best of all his sons, for he was the child of his old age; and he had made him a long ornamented tunic. When his brothers saw that their father loved him best of all his brothers, they hated him so much that they could not say a kind word to him.

Once Joseph had a dream, and when he told his brothers, they hated him even more. He said to them, "Listen to this dream I had. There we were, binding sheaves in the field, when suddenly my sheaf rose to an upright position, and your sheaves formed a ring around my sheaf and bowed down to it." His brothers said to him, "Are you really going to make yourself king over us? Will you rule over us?" So they hated him all the more because of his dreams and his reports.

Then he had another dream, and told it to his brothers. "Look, I had another dream," he said; "this time, the sun and the moon and eleven stars were bowing down to me." When he told it to his father and his brothers, his father reproved him and asked, "What is the meaning of this dream of yours? Can it be that I and your mother and your brothers are to come and bow to the ground before you?" So his brothers were furious at him but his father kept the matter in mind.

One day, when his brothers had gone to pasture their father's flocks at Shechem, Israel said to Joseph, "Are your brothers not tending our flocks at Shechem? Come and I will send you to them." "I am ready," Joseph answered. "Go then," he replied; "see if all is well with your brothers and the flocks, and bring back word." So he sent him off from the valley of Hebron. When Joseph reached Shechem, a man came upon him as he was wandering about in the fields. "What are you looking for?" the man asked him. "I am looking for my brothers," he answered. "Please tell me where they are tending the flocks." The man told him, "They have moved on from here; in fact, I heard them say, 'Let us go on to Dothan.'" So Joseph went after his brothers and found them

in Dothan. They saw him from a distance, and before he reached them, they plotted to kill him. They said to one another: "Here comes that dreamer! Come now, let us kill him and throw him into one of the cisterns here; we could say that a wild beast devoured him. We will see then what comes of his dreams." But when Reuben heard this, he tried to save him from their hands, saying: "We must not take his life." Then Reuben said, "Do not shed blood! Throw him into this cistern in the wilderness; but do not lay a hand on him." His purpose was to save him from their hands and restore him to his father.

So when Joseph came up to his brothers, they stripped him of his tunic, the long ornamented tunic he had on; then they took him and threw him into the cistern. The cistern was empty; there was no water in it.

Then they sat down to eat. Looking up, they saw a caravan of Ishmaelites coming from Gilead, their camels laden with gum, balm, and resin to be taken down to Egypt. Judah said to his brothers: "What is to be gained by killing our brother and concealing his blood? Come, let us sell him to these Ishmaelites, instead of doing away with him ourselves. After all, he is our brother, our own flesh." His brothers agreed. Midianite traders passed by, and they pulled Joseph up out of the cistern. They sold Joseph for twenty pieces of silver to the Ishmaelites, who took him to Egypt. —*Genesis 37:2–28*

"I am Joseph," he said to his brothers. "Is my father still alive?" But his brothers could give him no answer, so dumbfounded were they at him.

"Come closer to me," Joseph told his brothers. When they had done so, he said: "I am your brother Joseph, whom you sold into Egypt. But now do not be distressed, and do not be angry with yourselves for having sold me here. It was really for the sake of saving lives that God sent me here ahead of you. The famine has been in the land for two years now, and for five more years cultivation will yield no harvest. God, therefore, sent me on ahead of you to ensure for you a remnant on earth and to save your lives in an extraordinary deliverance. So it was not really you but God who had me come here; and he has made me a father to Pharaoh, LORD of all his household, and ruler over the whole land of Egypt." —*Genesis 45:3–8*

God's word strikes the heart. What word or phrase touched your heart?

_____

_____

_____

Joseph was probably tempted to give up and wonder why God had let such terrible things happen...but Joseph trusted God anyway. Looking back, how does Joseph understand all the bad things that God allowed to occur in his life?

_____

_____

_____

Use this space to sketch or doodle the symbol for the Scripture—COAT OF MANY COLORS

Describe a struggle in your life that eventually resulted in something good.

_____

_____

_____

In prayer, ask God to help you see and trust Him when life is hard. Write down what you hear Him say to you.

_____
_____
_____
_____
_____
_____

day 8   Exodus 2:23-3:17

God Calls Moses

A long time passed, during which the king of Egypt died. The Israelites groaned under their bondage and cried out, and from their bondage their cry for help went up to God. God heard their moaning and God was mindful of his covenanth with Abraham, Isaac and Jacob. God saw the Israelites, and God knew....

Meanwhile Moses was tending the flock of his father-in-law Jethro, the priest of Midian. Leading the flock beyond the wilderness, he came to the mountain of God, Horeb. There the angel of the LORD appeared to him as fire flaming out of a bush. When he looked, although the bush was on fire, it was not being consumed. So Moses decided, "I must turn aside to look at this remarkable sight. Why does the bush not burn up?" When the LORD saw that he had turned aside to look, God called out to him from the bush: Moses! Moses! He answered, "Here I am." God said: Do not come near! Remove your sandals from your feet, for the place where you stand is holy ground. I am the God of your father, he continued, the God of Abraham, the God of Isaac, and the God of Jacob.c Moses hid his face, for he was afraid to look at God.

But the LORD said: I have witnessed the affliction of my people in Egypt and have heard their cry against their taskmasters, so I know well what they are suffering. Therefore I have come down to rescue them from the power of the Egyptians and lead them up from that land into a good and spacious land, a land flowing with milk and honey, the country of the Canaanites, the Hittites, the Amorites, the Perizzites, the Girgashites, the Hivites and the Jebusites. Now indeed the outcry of the Israelites has reached me, and I have seen how the Egyptians are oppressing them. Now, go! I am sending you to Pharaoh to bring my people, the Israelites, out of Egypt.

But Moses said to God, "Who am I that I should go to Pharaoh and bring the Israelites out of Egypt?" God answered: I will be with you; and this will be your sign that I have sent you. When you have brought the people out of Egypt, you will serve God at this mountain. "But," said Moses to God, "if I go to the Israelites and say to them, 'The God of your ancestors has sent me to you,' and they ask me, 'What is his name?' what do I tell them?" God replied to Moses: I am who I am. Then he added: This is what you will tell the Israelites: I AM has sent me to you.

God spoke further to Moses: This is what you will say to the Israelites: The LORD, the God of your ancestors, the God of Abraham, the God of Isaac, and the God of Jacob, has sent me to you.

This is my name forever;
  this is my title for all generations.

Go and gather the elders of the Israelites, and tell them, The LORD, the God of your ancestors, the God of Abraham, Isaac, and Jacob, has appeared to me and said: I have observed you and what is being done to you in Egypt; so I have decided to lead you up out of your affliction in Egypt into the land of the Canaanites, the Hittites, the Amorites, the Perizzites, the Girgashites, the Hivites and the Jebusites, a land flowing with milk and honey.

God's word strikes the heart. What word or phrase touched your heart?

_____

_____

_____

Moses met God while he was watching the sheep. Why do you think God often likes to come to us in the ordinary moments of our day?

_____

_____

_____

Use this space to sketch or doodle the symbol for the Scripture—BURNING BUSH

Moses sees God in a bush that is on fire and yet still remains alive and green. Why do you think a fire that burns, but doesn't destroy, is used as an image for God?

_____

_____

Write a prayer asking God to help you see His presence in the ordinary moments of this day.

_____
_____
_____
_____
_____
_____

day 9   *Exodus 16:1-15, 35*

God Feeds His People

Having set out from Elim, the whole Israelite community came into the wilderness of Sin, which is between Elim and Sinai, on the fifteenth day of the second month after their departure from the land of Egypt. Here in the wilderness the whole Israelite community grumbled against Moses and Aaron. The Israelites said to them, "If only we had died at the LORD's hand in the land of Egypt, as we sat by our kettles of meat and ate our fill of bread! But you have led us into this wilderness to make this whole assembly die of famine!"

Then the LORD said to Moses: I am going to rain down bread from heaven for you. Each day the people are to go out and gather their daily portion; thus will I test them, to see whether they follow my instructions or not. On the sixth day, however, when they prepare what they bring in, let it be twice as much as they gather on the other days. So Moses and Aaron told all the Israelites, "At evening you will know that it was the LORD who brought you out of the land of Egypt; and in the morning you will see the glory of the LORD, when he hears your grumbling against him. But who are we that you should grumble against us?" And Moses said, "When the LORD gives you meat to eat in the evening and in the morning your fill of bread, and hears the grumbling you utter against him, who then are we? Your grumbling is not against us, but against the LORD."

Then Moses said to Aaron, "Tell the whole Israelite community: Approach the LORD, for he has heard your grumbling." But while Aaron was speaking to the whole Israelite community, they turned in the direction of the wilderness, and there the glory of the LORD appeared in the cloud! The LORD said to Moses: I have heard the grumbling of the Israelites. Tell them: In the evening twilight you will eat meat, and in the morning you will have your fill of bread, and then you will know that I, the LORD, am your God.

In the evening, quail came up and covered the camp. In the morning there was a layer of dew all about the camp, and when the layer of dew evaporated, fine flakes were on the surface of the wilderness, fine flakes like hoarfrost on the ground. On seeing it, the Israelites asked one another, "What is this?" for they did not know what it was. But Moses told them, "It is the bread which the LORD has given you to eat. —*Exodus 16:1–15*

The Israelites ate the manna for forty years, until they came to settled land; they ate the manna until they came to the borders of Canaan. —*Exodus 16:35*

But Moses told them, " It is the bread which

the LORD has given you to eat."

Exodus 16:15

God's word strikes the heart. What word or phrase touched your heart?

_____
_____

What are some things you usually complain about? Do you think your complaining is a good thing? If yes, why? If no, how could you change?

_____
_____
_____

Use this space to sketch or doodle the symbol for the Scripture—MANNA and QUAIL

Even though the Israelites grumbled and complained, God still fed them for the next forty years. Is there anyone in your life who seems to be always grumbling and taking your energy? How might you be called to show your love for them anyway?

_____
_____

Write a prayer for someone who often bothers you or whom you struggle to like.

_____
_____
_____
_____
_____
_____

day 10 *Exodus 19:1-11, 20:1-17*

God Gives Moses His Laws

In the third month after the Israelites' departure from the land of Egypt, on the first day, they came to the wilderness of Sinai. After they made the journey from Rephidim and entered the wilderness of Sinai, they then pitched camp in the wilderness.

While Israel was encamped there in front of the mountain, Moses went up to the mountain of God. Then the LORD called to him from the mountain, saying: This is what you will say to the house of Jacob; tell the Israelites: You have seen how I treated the Egyptians and how I bore you up on eagles' wings and brought you to myself. Now, if you obey me completely and keep my covenant, you will be my treasured possession among all peoples, though all the earth is mine. You will be to me a kingdom of priests, a holy nation. That is what you must tell the Israelites. So Moses went and summoned the elders of the people. When he set before them all that the LORD had ordered him to tell them, all the people answered together, "Everything the LORD has said, we will do." Then Moses brought back to the LORD the response of the people.

The LORD said to Moses: I am coming to you now in a dense cloud, so that when the people hear me speaking with you, they will also remain faithful to you.

When Moses, then, had reported the response of the people to the LORD, the LORD said to Moses: Go to the people and have them sanctify themselves today and tomorrow. Have them wash their garments and be ready for the third day; for on the third day the LORD will come down on Mount Sinai in the sight of all the people. —*Exodus 19:1–11*

Then God spoke all these words:

I am the LORD your God, who brought you out of the land of Egypt, out of the house of slavery. You shall not have other gods beside me. You shall not make for yourself an idol or a likeness of anything in the heavens above or on the earth below or in the waters beneath the earth; you shall not bow

down before them or serve them. For I, the LORD, your God, am a jealous God, inflicting punishment for their ancestors' wickedness on the children of those who hate me, down to the third and fourth generation; but showing love down to the thousandth generation of those who love me and keep my commandments.

You shall not invoke the name of the LORD, your God, in vain. For the LORD will not leave unpunished anyone who invokes his name in vain.

Remember the sabbath day—keep it holy. Six days you may labor and do all your work, but the seventh day is a sabbath of the LORD your God. You shall not do any work, either you, your son or your daughter, your male or female slave, your work animal, or the resident alien within your gates. For in six days the LORD made the heavens and the earth, the sea and all that is in them; but on the seventh day he rested. That is why the LORD has blessed the sabbath day and made it holy.

Honor your father and your mother, that you may have a long life in the land the LORD your God is giving you.

You shall not kill.
You shall not commit adultery.
You shall not steal.
You shall not bear false witness against your neighbor.
You shall not covet your neighbor's house. You shall not covet your neighbor's wife, his male or female slave, his ox or donkey, or anything that belongs to your neighbor. —*Exodus 20:1–17*

God's word strikes the heart. What word or phrase touched your heart?

God sees us as His treasured possessions. In response to His love, God asks that we keep the commandments. Which commandment do you find the most difficult? Why is this commandment challenging for you?

Use this space to sketch or doodle the symbol for the Scripture—STONE TABLETS

Which commandment comes easy to you?

In prayer, ask God how He wants you to be holy. Write down what He says to you.

_____
_____
_____
_____
_____
_____

day 11 Joshua 6:1-20

Wall of Jericho Falls

Now Jericho was in a state of siege because of the presence of the Israelites. No one left or entered. And to Joshua the LORD said: I have delivered Jericho, its king, and its warriors into your power. Have all the soldiers circle the city, marching once around it. Do this for six days, with seven priests carrying ram's horns ahead of the ark. On the seventh day march around the city seven times, and have the priests blow the horns. When they give a long blast on the ram's horns and you hear the sound of the horn, all the people shall shout aloud. The wall of the city will collapse, and the people shall attack straight ahead.

Summoning the priests, Joshua, son of Nun, said to them, "Take up the ark of the covenant with seven of the priests carrying ram's horns in front of the ark of the LORD." And he ordered the people, "Proceed and surround the city, with the picked troops marching ahead of the ark of the LORD." When Joshua spoke to the people, the seven priests who carried the ram's horns before the LORD marched and blew their horns, and the ark of the covenant of the LORD followed them. In front of the priests with the horns marched the picked troops; the rear guard followed the ark, and the blowing of horns was kept up continually as they marched. But Joshua had commanded the people, "Do not shout or make any noise or outcry until I tell you, 'Shout!' Then you must shout." So he had the ark of the LORD circle the city, going once around it, after which they returned to camp for the night.

Early the next morning, Joshua had the priests take up the ark of the LORD. The seven priests bearing the ram's horns marched in front of the ark of the LORD, blowing their horns. Ahead of these marched the picked troops, while the rear guard followed the ark of the LORD, and the blowing of horns was kept up continually. On this second day they again marched around the city once before returning to camp; and for six days in all they did the same.

On the seventh day, beginning at daybreak, they marched around the city seven times in the same manner; on that day only did they march around the city seven times. The seventh time around, the priests blew the horns and

Joshua said to the people, "Now shout, for the LORD has given you the city. The city and everything in it is under the ban. Only Rahab the prostitute and all who are in the house with her are to live, because she hid the messengers we sent. But be careful not to covet or take anything that is under the ban; otherwise you will bring upon the camp of Israel this ban and the misery of it. All silver and gold, and the articles of bronze or iron, are holy to the LORD. They shall be put in the treasury of the LORD."

As the horns blew, the people began to shout. When they heard the sound of the horn, they raised a tremendous shout. The wall collapsed, and the people attacked the city straight ahead and took it.

God's word strikes the heart. What word or phrase touched your heart?

_____

_____

_____

Walking around the city time after time, Joshua probably felt a little foolish. Have you ever felt foolish as you try to live as a disciple of Christ? Why or why not?

_____

_____

_____

Use this space to sketch or doodle the symbol for the Scripture—HORNS

The Israelites brought the ark of the Lord into battle with them. What is one area of your life that you would like God to come and help you with?

_____

_____

_____

Write a prayer expressing your willingness to be foolish and/or suffer for God.

_____
_____
_____
_____
_____
_____

day 12 Ruth 1:1–18

Ruth Helps Naomi

Once back in the time of the judges there was a famine in the land; so a man from Bethlehem of Judah left home with his wife and two sons to reside on the plateau of Moab. The man was named Elimelech, his wife Naomi, and his sons Mahlon and Chilion; they were Ephrathites from Bethlehem of Judah. Some time after their arrival on the plateau of Moab, Elimelech, the husband of Naomi, died, and she was left with her two sons. They married Moabite women, one named Orpah, the other Ruth. When they had lived there about ten years, both Mahlon and Chilion died also, and the woman was left with neither her two boys nor her husband.

She and her daughters-in-law then prepared to go back from the plateau of Moab because word had reached her there that the LORD had seen to his people's needs and given them food. She and her two daughters-in-law left the place where they had been living. On the road back to the land of Judah, Naomi said to her daughters-in-law, "Go back, each of you to your mother's house. May the LORD show you the same kindness as you have shown to the deceased and to me. May the LORD guide each of you to find a husband and a home in which you will be at rest." She kissed them good-bye, but they wept aloud, crying, "No! We will go back with you, to your people." Naomi replied, "Go back, my daughters. Why come with me? Have I other sons in my womb who could become your husbands? Go, my daughters, for I am too old to marry again. Even if I had any such hope, or if tonight I had a husband and were to bear sons, would you wait for them and deprive yourselves of husbands until those sons grew up? No, my daughters, my lot is too bitter for you, because the LORD has extended his hand against me." Again they wept aloud; then Orpah kissed her mother-in-law good-bye, but Ruth clung to her.

"See now," she said, "your sister-in-law has gone back to her people and her god. Go back after your sister-in-law!" But Ruth said, "Do not press me to go back and abandon you!

Wherever you go I will go,
  wherever you lodge I will lodge.
Your people shall be my people
  and your God, my God.
Where you die I will die,
  and there be buried.

May the LORD do thus to me, and more, if even death separates me from you!" Naomi then ceased to urge her, for she saw she was determined to go with her.

God's word strikes the heart. What word or phrase touched your heart?

_____

_____

Ruth is a true friend to Naomi. Give an example of how someone has been a true friend to you.

_____

_____

Use this space to sketch or doodle the symbol for the Scripture—BUSHEL OF WHEAT

Naomi doesn't want Ruth to suffer, so she tells her to return home to her own people. However, Ruth's love for Naomi is greater than her fear of future suffering. She decides to stay with Naomi. Describe a time that you were willing to suffer because of your love for another person.

_____

_____

Reflect on the ways God has been a friend to you. Write some of them down and thank God for being there for you in good times and hard times.

___

___

___

___

___

___

day 13 — 1 Samuel 3:1-21

God Calls Samuel

During the time young Samuel was minister to the LORD under Eli, the word of the LORD was scarce and vision infrequent. One day Eli was asleep in his usual place. His eyes had lately grown so weak that he could not see. The lamp of God was not yet extinguished, and Samuel was sleeping in the temple of the LORD where the ark of God was. The LORD called to Samuel, who answered, "Here I am." He ran to Eli and said, "Here I am. You called me." "I did not call you," Eli answered. "Go back to sleep." So he went back to sleep. Again the LORD called Samuel, who rose and went to Eli. "Here I am," he said. "You called me." But he answered, "I did not call you, my son. Go back to sleep."

Samuel did not yet recognize the LORD, since the word of the LORD had not yet been revealed to him. The LORD called Samuel again, for the third time. Getting up and going to Eli, he said, "Here I am. You called me." Then Eli understood that the LORD was calling the youth. So he said to Samuel, "Go to sleep, and if you are called, reply, 'Speak, LORD, for your servant is listening.'" When Samuel went to sleep in his place, the LORD came and stood there, calling out as before: Samuel, Samuel! Samuel answered, "Speak, for your servant is listening." The LORD said to Samuel: I am about to do something in Israel that will make the ears of everyone who hears it ring. On that day I will carry out against Eli everything I have said about his house, beginning to end. I announce to him that I am condemning his house once and for all, because of this crime: though he knew his sons were blaspheming God, he did not reprove them. Therefore, I swear to Eli's house: No sacrifice or offering will ever expiate its crime. Samuel then slept until morning, when he got up early and opened the doors of the temple of the LORD. He was afraid to tell Eli the vision, but Eli called to him, "Samuel, my son!" He replied, "Here I am." Then Eli asked, "What did he say to you? Hide nothing from me! May God do thus to you, and more, if you hide from me a single thing he told you." So Samuel told him everything, and held nothing back. Eli answered, "It is the LORD. What is pleasing in the LORD's sight, the LORD will do."

Samuel grew up, and the LORD was with him, not permitting any word of his to go unfulfilled. Thus all Israel from Dan to Beer-sheba came to know that Samuel was a trustworthy prophet of the LORD. The LORD continued to appear at Shiloh, manifesting himself to Samuel at Shiloh through his word. Samuel's word spread throughout Israel.

God's word strikes the heart. What word or phrase touched your heart?

_____
_____
_____

God often speaks to us when we least expect it. Knowing that God communicates in many ways, in what ways do you think God might speak to you today?

_____
_____
_____

Use this space to sketch or doodle the symbol for the Scripture—BOY SLEEPING

God spoke to Samuel in the temple. Why does God often like to speak to us at Mass or in the quiet of the church?

_____
_____
_____
_____

In prayer, repeat Samuel's words, "Speak, Lord. Your servant is listening." Write down what God says to you.

_____
_____
_____
_____
_____
_____

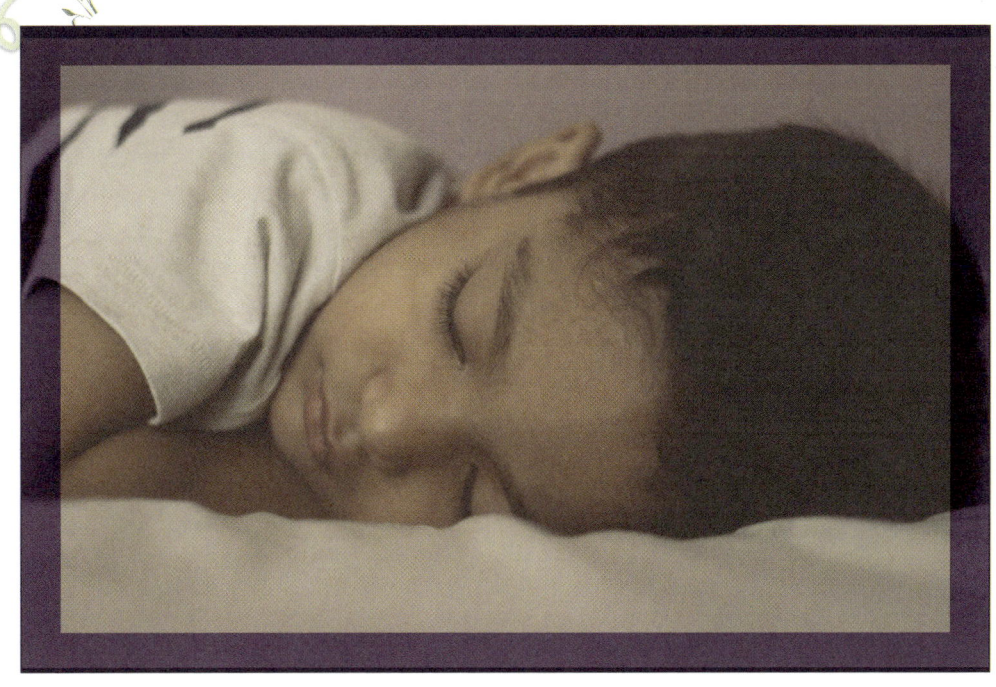

day 14 *1 Samuel 16:1-13*

Jesse's Family Is Chosen

The LORD said to Samuel: How long will you grieve for Saul, whom I have rejected as king of Israel? Fill your horn with oil, and be on your way. I am sending you to Jesse of Bethlehem, for from among his sons I have decided on a king. But Samuel replied: "How can I go? Saul will hear of it and kill me." To this the LORD answered: Take a heifer along and say, "I have come to sacrifice to the LORD." Invite Jesse to the sacrifice, and I myself will tell you what to do; you are to anoint for me the one I point out to you.

Samuel did as the LORD had commanded him. When he entered Bethlehem, the elders of the city came trembling to meet him and asked, "Is your visit peaceful, O seer?" He replied: "Yes! I have come to sacrifice to the LORD. So purify yourselves and celebrate with me today." He also had Jesse and his sons purify themselves and invited them to the sacrifice. As they came, he looked at Eliab and thought, "Surely the anointed is here before the LORD." But the LORD said to Samuel: Do not judge from his appearance or from his lofty stature, because I have rejected him. God does not see as a mortal, who sees the appearance. The LORD looks into the heart. Then Jesse called Abinadab and presented him before Samuel, who said, "The LORD has not chosen him." Next Jesse presented Shammah, but Samuel said, "The LORD has not chosen this one either." In the same way Jesse presented seven sons before Samuel, but Samuel said to Jesse, "The LORD has not chosen any one of these." Then Samuel asked Jesse, "Are these all the sons you have?" Jesse replied, "There is still the youngest, but he is tending the sheep." Samuel said to Jesse, "Send for him; we will not sit down to eat until he arrives here." Jesse had the young man brought to them. He was ruddy, a youth with beautiful eyes, and good looking. The LORD said: There—anoint him, for this is the one! Then Samuel, with the horn of oil in hand, anointed him in the midst of his brothers, and from that day on, the spirit of the LORD rushed upon David. Then Samuel set out for Ramah.

Then Samuel, with the horn of oil in hand, anointed him

in the midst of his brothers, and from that day on, the

spirit of the LORD rushed upon David.

1 Samuel 16:13

God's word strikes the heart. What word or phrase touched your heart?

_____

_____

_____

Why do we often judge other people by appearances? What might it take to see others as God does?

_____

_____

_____

Use this space to sketch or doodle the symbol for the Scripture—BRANCH GROWING FROM STUMP

How does God choose His leaders? If He looked into your heart, do you think He would see someone who could lead others? If yes, why? If no, what needs to change?

_____

_____

_____

Write a prayer asking God to forgive you for judging people by appearances. Ask God to help you see people as He does.

_____
_____
_____
_____
_____
_____

day 15 *1 Samuel 17:1, 4, 8-11, 32-37, 40-51*

David Kills Goliath

The Philistines rallied their forces for battle at Socoh in Judah and camped between Socoh and Azekah at Ephes-dammim. —*1 Samuel 17:1*

A champion named Goliath of Gath came out from the Philistine camp; he was six cubits and a span tall. —*1 Samuel 17:4*

He stood and shouted to the ranks of Israel: "Why come out in battle formation? I am a Philistine, and you are Saul's servants. Choose one of your men, and have him come down to me. If he beats me in combat and kills me, we will be your vassals; but if I beat him and kill him, you shall be our vassals and serve us." The Philistine continued: "I defy the ranks of Israel today. Give me a man and let us fight together." When Saul and all Israel heard this challenge of the Philistine, they were stunned and terrified. —*1 Samuel 17:8–11*

Then David spoke to Saul: "My lord should not lose heart. Let your servant go and fight this Philistine." But Saul answered David, "You cannot go up against this Philistine and fight with him, for you are only a youth, while he has been a warrior from his youth." Then David told Saul: "Your servant used to tend his father's sheep, and whenever a lion or bear came to carry off a sheep from the flock, I would chase after it, attack it, and snatch the prey from its mouth. If it attacked me, I would seize it by the throat, strike it, and kill it. Your servant has killed both a lion and a bear. This uncircumcised Philistine will be as one of them, because he has insulted the armies of the living God."

David continued: "The same LORD who delivered me from the claws of the lion and the bear will deliver me from the hand of this Philistine." Saul answered David, "Go! the LORD will be with you."
—*1 Samuel 17:32–37*

Then, staff in hand, David selected five smooth stones from the wadi and put them in the pocket of his shepherd's bag. With his sling in hand, he approached the Philistine.

With his shield-bearer marching before him, the Philistine advanced closer and closer to David. When he sized David up and saw that he was youthful, ruddy, and handsome in appearance, he began to deride him. He said to David, "Am I a dog that you come against me with a staff?" Then the Philistine cursed David by his gods and said to him, "Come here to me, and I will feed your flesh to the birds of the air and the beasts of the field." David answered him: "You come against me with sword and spear and scimitar, but I come against you in the name of the LORD of hosts, the God of the armies of Israel whom you have insulted. Today the LORD shall deliver you into my hand; I will strike you down and cut off your head. This very day I will feed your dead body and the dead bodies of the Philistine army to the birds of the air and the beasts of the field; thus the whole land shall learn that Israel has a God. All this multitude, too, shall learn that it is not by sword or spear that the LORD saves. For the battle belongs to the LORD, who shall deliver you into our hands."

The Philistine then moved to meet David at close quarters, while David ran quickly toward the battle line to meet the Philistine. David put his hand into the bag and took out a stone, hurled it with the sling, and struck the Philistine on the forehead. The stone embedded itself in his brow, and he fell on his face to the ground. Thus David triumphed over the Philistine with sling and stone; he struck the Philistine dead, and did it without a sword in his hand. Then David ran and stood over him; with the Philistine's own sword which he drew from its sheath he killed him, and cut off his head. —*1 Samuel 17:40–51*

God's word strikes the heart. What word or phrase touched your heart?

_____
_____
_____

Why does David see the situation with Goliath differently than the king and his men? Why is David so confident and unafraid?

_____
_____
_____
_____

Use this space to sketch or doodle the symbol for the Scripture—SLING and STONE

Is David a better example of the virtue of courage or of trust? Explain.

_____
_____
_____

Write a prayer expressing your confidence in God. If you would like to see an example, read Psalm 23, David's prayer of confidence in God.

_____
_____
_____
_____
_____
_____

day 16 1 Kings 3:5-28

Solomon's Wisdom

In Gibeon the LORD appeared to Solomon in a dream at night. God said: Whatever you ask I shall give you. Solomon answered: "You have shown great kindness to your servant, David my father, because he walked before you with fidelity, justice, and an upright heart; and you have continued this great kindness toward him today, giving him a son to sit upon his throne. Now, LORD, my God, you have made me, your servant, king to succeed David my father; but I am a mere youth, not knowing at all how to act—I, your servant, among the people you have chosen, a people so vast that it cannot be numbered or counted. Give your servant, therefore, a listening heart to judge your people and to distinguish between good and evil. For who is able to give judgment for this vast people of yours?"

The LORD was pleased by Solomon's request. So God said to him: Because you asked for this—you did not ask for a long life for yourself, nor for riches, nor for the life of your enemies—but you asked for discernment to know what is right—I now do as you request. I give you a heart so wise and discerning that there has never been anyone like you until now, nor after you will there be anyone to equal you. In addition, I give you what you have not asked for: I give you such riches and glory that among kings there will be no one like you all your days. And if you walk in my ways, keeping my statutes and commandments, as David your father did, I will give you a long life. Solomon awoke; it was a dream! He went to Jerusalem, stood before the ark of the covenant of the LORD, sacrificed burnt offerings and communion offerings, and gave a feast for all his servants.

Later, two prostitutes came to the king and stood before him. One woman said: "By your leave, my LORD, this woman and I live in the same house, and I gave birth in the house while she was present. On the third day after I gave birth, this woman also gave birth. We were alone; no one else was in the house with us; only the two of us were in the house. This woman's son died during the night when she lay on top of him. So in the middle of the night she got up and took my son from my side, as your servant was sleeping. Then she laid him in her bosom and laid her dead son in my bosom. I rose in the morning to nurse my son, and he was dead! But when I examined him in the morning light, I saw it was not the son I had borne." The other woman answered, "No! The living one is my son, the dead one is yours." But the first kept saying, "No! the dead one is your son, the living one is mine!" Thus they argued before the king. Then the king said: "One woman claims, 'This, the living one, is my son, the dead one is yours.' The other answers, 'No! The dead one is your son, the living one is mine.'" The king continued, "Get me a sword." When they brought the sword before the king, he said, "Cut the living child in two, and give half to one woman and half to the other." The woman whose son was alive, because she was stirred with compassion for her son, said to the king, "Please, my lord, give her the living baby—do not kill it!" But the other said, "It shall be neither mine nor yours. Cut it in two!" The king then answered, "Give her the living baby! Do not kill it! She is the mother." When all Israel heard the judgment the king had given, they were in awe of him, because they saw that the king had in him the wisdom of God for giving right judgment.

God's word strikes the heart. What word or phrase touched your heart?

Solomon asked God for a "listening heart." What is a listening heart and why is it important?

Use this space to sketch or doodle the symbol for the Scripture—LIGHT (Torch)

In his wisdom, Solomon is able to discern the real mother by the depths of her love. Solomon realizes that real love is willing to sacrifice for the beloved. As you prepare for Christmas, what are two or three things you can sacrifice for Jesus this week?

In prayer, ask God for a listening heart. Write down what He says to you.

_____
_____
_____
_____
_____
_____

day 17 2 Kings 2:1-13

God Takes Elijah to Heaven

When the LORD was about to take Elijah up to heaven in a whirlwind, he and Elisha were on their way from Gilgal.

Elijah said to Elisha, "Stay here, please. The LORD has sent me on to Bethel." Elisha replied, "As the LORD lives, and as you yourself live, I will not leave you." So they went down to Bethel. The guild prophets who were in Bethel went out to Elisha and asked him, "Do you know that today the LORD will take your master from you?" He replied, "Yes, I know that. Be still."

Elijah said to him, "Elisha, stay here, please. The LORD has sent me on to Jericho." Elisha replied, "As the LORD lives, and as you yourself live, I will not leave you." So they came to Jericho. The guild prophets who were in Jericho approached Elisha and asked him, "Do you know that today the LORD will take your master from you?" He replied, "Yes, I know that. Be still."

Elijah said to him, "Stay here, please. The LORD has sent me on to the Jordan." Elisha replied, "As the LORD lives, and as you yourself live, I will not leave you." So the two went on together. Fifty of the guild prophets followed and stood facing them at a distance, while the two of them stood next to the Jordan.

Elijah took his mantle, rolled it up and struck the water: it divided, and the two of them crossed over on dry ground.

When they had crossed over, Elijah said to Elisha, "Request whatever I might do for you, before I am taken from you." Elisha answered, "May I receive a double portion of your spirit." He replied, "You have asked something that is not easy. Still, if you see me taken up from you, your wish will be granted; otherwise not." As they walked on still conversing, a fiery chariot and fiery horses came between the two of them, and Elijah went up to heaven in a whirlwind, and Elisha saw it happen. He cried out, "My father! my father! Israel's chariot and steeds!" Then he saw him no longer.

He gripped his own garment, tore it into two pieces, and picked up the mantle which had fallen from Elijah. Then he went back and stood at the bank of the Jordan.

A fiery chariot and fiery horses came between the two of them,

and Elijah went up to heaven in a whirlwind,

and Elisha saw it happen.

2 Kings: 2: 11–12

God's word strikes the heart. What word or phrase touched your heart?

_____
_____
_____

Elisha was one of Elijah's disciples. How did Elisha show his love for Elijah and all that Elijah had taught him?

_____
_____
_____

Use this space to sketch or doodle the symbol for the Scripture—CHARIOT OF FIRE

As you strive to be a disciple of Christ, what lesson can you learn from the example of the disciple Elisha?

_____
_____
_____

In prayer, ask God how you can be a better disciple. Write down what He says to you.

___
___
___
___
___
___
___

day 18 Daniel 6:4-5, 7-13, 17-28
Daniel in the Lion's Den

Daniel outshone all the ministers and satraps because an extraordinary spirit was in him, and the king considered setting him over the entire kingdom. Then the ministers and satraps tried to find grounds for accusation against Daniel regarding the kingdom. But they could not accuse him of any corruption. Because he was trustworthy, no fault or corruption was to be found in him. —
Daniel 6:4–5

So these ministers and satraps stormed in to the king and said to him, "King Darius, live forever! All the ministers of the kingdom, the prefects, satraps, counselors, and governors agree that the following prohibition ought to be put in force by royal decree: for thirty days, whoever makes a petition to anyone, divine or human, except to you, O king, shall be thrown into a den of lions. Now, O king, let the prohibition be issued over your signature, immutable and irrevocable according to the law of the Medes and Persians." So King Darius signed the prohibition into law.

Even after Daniel heard that this law had been signed, he continued his custom of going home to kneel in prayer and give thanks to his God in the upper chamber three times a day, with the windows open toward Jerusalem. So these men stormed in and found Daniel praying and pleading before his God. Then they went to remind the king about the prohibition: "Did you not sign a decree, O king, that for thirty days, whoever makes a petition to anyone, divine or human, except to you, O king, shall be cast into a den of lions?" The king answered them, "The decree is absolute, irrevocable under the law of the Medes and Persians."
—Daniel 6:7–13

So the king ordered Daniel to be brought and cast into the lions' den. To Daniel he said, "Your God, whom you serve so constantly, must save you." To forestall any tampering, the king sealed with his own ring and the rings of the lords the stone that had been brought to block the opening of the den.

Then the king returned to his palace for the night; he refused to eat and he dismissed the entertainers. Since sleep was impossible for him, the king rose

very early the next morning and hastened to the lions' den. As he drew near, he cried out to Daniel sorrowfully, "Daniel, servant of the living God, has your God whom you serve so constantly been able to save you from the lions?" Daniel answered the king: "O king, live forever! My God sent his angel and closed the lions' mouths so that they have not hurt me. For I have been found innocent before him; neither have I done you any harm, O king!" This gave the king great joy. At his order Daniel was brought up from the den; he was found to be unharmed because he trusted in his God. The king then ordered the men who had accused Daniel, along with their children and their wives, to be cast into the lions' den. Before they reached the bottom of the den, the lions overpowered them and crushed all their bones.

Then King Darius wrote to the nations and peoples of every language, wherever they dwell on the earth: "May your peace abound! I decree that throughout my royal domain the God of Daniel is to be reverenced and feared:

"For he is the living God, enduring forever,
  whose kingdom shall not
    be destroyed,
  whose dominion shall be
    without end,
A savior and deliverer,
  working signs and wonders in heaven
    and on earth,
  who saved Daniel from the
    lions' power." —*Daniel 6:17–28*

God's word strikes the heart. What word or phrase touched your heart?

God's sends His angel to protect Daniel from the lions. Think of one challenge you will need to face in the next few days. Write a short prayer below, asking your guardian angel to be with you when the challenge comes.

Use this space to sketch or doodle the symbol for the Scripture—LION

King Darius lists several qualities of God. Which is your favorite quality and why?

Write a prayer praising God. In your prayer, list several qualities of God.

_____
_____
_____
_____
_____
_____

day 19 Jonah 1:1-15, 2:1-11

Jonah in the Whale

The word of the LORD came to Jonah, son of Amittai: Set out for the great city of Nineveh, and preach against it; for their wickedness has come before me. But Jonah made ready to flee to Tarshish, away from the LORD. He went down to Joppa, found a ship going to Tarshish, paid the fare, and went down in it to go with them to Tarshish, away from the LORD.

The LORD, however, hurled a great wind upon the sea, and the storm was so great that the ship was about to break up. Then the sailors were afraid and each one cried to his god. To lighten the ship for themselves, they threw its cargo into the sea. Meanwhile, Jonah had gone down into the hold of the ship, and lay there fast asleep. The captain approached him and said, "What are you doing asleep? Get up, call on your god! Perhaps this god will be mindful of us so that we will not perish."

Then they said to one another, "Come, let us cast lots to discover on whose account this evil has come to us." So they cast lots, and the lot fell on Jonah. They said to him, "Tell us why this evil has come to us! What is your business? Where do you come from? What is your country, and to what people do you belong?" "I am a Hebrew," he replied; "I fear the LORD, the God of heaven, who made the sea and the dry land."

Now the men were seized with great fear and said to him, "How could you do such a thing!"—They knew that he was fleeing from the LORD, because he had told them. They asked, "What shall we do with you, that the sea may calm down for us?" For the sea was growing more and more stormy. Jonah responded, "Pick me up and hurl me into the sea and then the sea will calm down for you. For I know that this great storm has come upon you because of me."

Still the men rowed hard to return to dry land, but they could not, for the sea grew more and more stormy. Then they cried to the LORD: "Please, O LORD, do not let us perish for taking this man's life; do not charge us with shedding innocent blood, for you, LORD, have accomplished what you desired." Then they picked up Jonah and hurled him into the sea, and the sea stopped raging. —*Jonah 1:1–15*

But the LORD sent a great fish to swallow Jonah, and he remained in the belly of the fish three days and three nights. Jonah prayed to the LORD, his God, from the belly of the fish:

Out of my distress I called to the LORD,
  and he answered me;
From the womb of Sheol I cried
    for help,
  and you heard my voice.
You cast me into the deep, into the
    heart of the sea,
  and the flood enveloped me;
All your breakers and your billows
  passed over me.
Then I said, "I am banished from
    your sight!
  How will I again look upon your
    holy temple?"
The waters surged around me up to
    my neck;
  the deep enveloped me;
  seaweed wrapped around my head.
I went down to the roots
    of the mountains;
  to the land whose bars closed behind
    me forever,
But you brought my life up from the pit,
  O LORD, my God.

When I became faint,
  I remembered the LORD;
My prayer came to you
  in your holy temple.
Those who worship worthless idols
  abandon their hope for mercy.
But I, with thankful voice,
  will sacrifice to you;
What I have vowed I will pay:
  deliverance is from the LORD.

Then the LORD commanded the fish to vomit Jonah upon dry land.
—Jonah 2:1–11

God's word strikes the heart. What word or phrase touched your heart?

_____
_____
_____

When God first reveals His will to Jonah, how does Jonah respond? Using the story of Jonah as an example, what is our life like if we choose to run away from God's will for us?

_____
_____
_____

Use this space to sketch or doodle the symbol for the Scripture—WHALE

How does Jonah's story show us that even if we run from God, God will always be with us?

_____
_____
_____

Write a prayer expressing your desire to do God's will right away, the first time you hear it.

_____
_____
_____
_____
_____

day 20 *Matthew 1:23; Isaiah 7:14*

The Blessed Virgin Mary

"Behold, the virgin shall be with child and bear a son,
 and they shall name him Emmanuel,"

which means "God is with us." —*Matthew 1:23*

Therefore the Lord himself will give you a sign; the young woman, pregnant and about to bear a son, shall name him Emmanuel. —*Isaiah 7:14*

"Behold, the virgin shall be with child and bear a son,

and they shall name him Emmanuel,"

which means "God is with us."

Matthew 1:23

God's word strikes the heart. What word or phrase touched your heart?

_____
_____
_____

For many people, the idea that God would become a human being, born of the Virgin Mary, and live among us on earth, is shocking. What is so stunning and incredible about the fact of "Emmanuel" or God is with us?

_____
_____
_____
_____

Use this space to sketch or doodle the symbol for the Scripture—WHITE ROSE

Why do people so easily forget that God is with us?

_____
_____
_____

Write a prayer expressing your longing to be aware of God's presence always and most especially this Christmas.

___
___
___
___
___
___

day 21 Luke 1:26–38

Gabriel Appears to Mary

The angel Gabriel was sent from God to a town of Galilee called Nazareth, to a virgin betrothed to a man named Joseph, of the house of David, and the virgin's name was Mary. And coming to her, he said, "Hail, favored one! The Lord is with you." But she was greatly troubled at what was said and pondered what sort of greeting this might be. Then the angel said to her, "Do not be afraid, Mary, for you have found favor with God. Behold, you will conceive in your womb and bear a son, and you shall name him Jesus. He will be great and will be called Son of the Most High, and the Lord God will give him the throne of David his father, and he will rule over the house of Jacob forever, and of his kingdom there will be no end." But Mary said to the angel, "How can this be, since I have no relations with a man?" And the angel said to her in reply, "The holy Spirit will come upon you, and the power of the Most High will overshadow you. Therefore the child to be born will be called holy, the Son of God. And behold, Elizabeth, your relative, has also conceived a son in her old age, and this is the sixth month for her who was called barren; for nothing will be impossible for God." Mary said, "Behold, I am the handmaid of the Lord. May it be done to me according to your word." Then the angel departed from her.

"Behold, I am the handmaid of the Lord.

May it be done to me according to your word."

Luke 1:38

God's word strikes the heart. What word or phrase touched your heart?

_____
_____
_____

Mary is the first and greatest of all Jesus' disciples. Based on the Scripture passage, how do you think Mary felt when the angel Gabriel appeared to her? What did Mary decide to do?

_____
_____
_____

Use this space to sketch or doodle the symbol for the Scripture—ANGEL

The Holy Spirit entered into Mary when she said yes to God. How would you like the Holy Spirit to come into your life?

_____
_____
_____
_____

Jesus came into the world through Mary. Write a prayer thanking God for the gift of His mother.

_____
_____
_____
_____
_____

day 22 *Matthew 1:18-25*

St. Joseph

Now this is how the birth of Jesus Christ came about. When his mother Mary was betrothed to Joseph, but before they lived together, she was found with child through the holy Spirit. Joseph her husband, since he was a righteous man, yet unwilling to expose her to shame, decided to divorce her quietly. Such was his intention when, behold, the angel of the Lord appeared to him in a dream and said, "Joseph, son of David, do not be afraid to take Mary your wife into your home. For it is through the holy Spirit that this child has been conceived in her. She will bear a son and you are to name him Jesus, because he will save his people from their sins." All this took place to fulfill what the Lord had said through the prophet:

> "Behold, the virgin shall be with child and bear a son,
> and they shall name him Emmanuel,"

which means "God is with us." When Joseph awoke, he did as the angel of the Lord had commanded him and took his wife into his home. He had no relations with her until she bore a son, and he named him Jesus.

"She will bear a son and you are to name him Jesus,

because he will save his people from their sins."

Matthew 1:21

God's word strikes the heart. What word or phrase touched your heart?

Joseph is a righteous/just man. What are the qualities of a just man? Why do you think God chose Joseph to be the husband of Mary and father of Jesus?

Use this space to sketch or doodle the symbol for the Scripture—CARPENTER'S TOOL

As Christmas approaches, how can you grow in the virtue of justice?

Joseph never speaks in Scripture. In prayer, ask Jesus why St. Joseph is silent. Write down what He says to you.

_____
_____
_____
_____
_____

day 23 Luke 2:1-7

Mary and Joseph Travel to Bethlehem

In those days a decree went out from Caesar Augustus that the whole world should be enrolled. This was the first enrollment, when Quirinius was governor of Syria. So all went to be enrolled, each to his own town. And Joseph too went up from Galilee from the town of Nazareth to Judea, to the city of David that is called Bethlehem, because he was of the house and family of David, to be enrolled with Mary, his betrothed, who was with child. While they were there, the time came for her to have her child, and she gave birth to her firstborn son. She wrapped him in swaddling clothes and laid him in a manger, because there was no room for them in the inn.

She wrapped him in swaddling clothes and

laid him in a manger because

there was no room for him at the inn.

Luke 2:7

God's word strikes the heart. What word or phrase touched your heart?

_____
_____
_____

Jesus could have lived in any type of home. Why do you think Jesus lived in poverty, not even having his own room when he was born?

_____
_____
_____

Use this space to sketch or doodle the symbol for the Scripture—MARY and JOSEPH ON A DONKEY

On Christmas, Jesus will be with each of us if we let him. How will Jesus know that your heart is open and has room for him?

_____
_____
_____

Write a prayer welcoming Jesus into your heart.

_____
_____
_____
_____
_____
_____
_____

day 24 Matthew 2:1-12

Wise Men Follow the Star

When Jesus was born in Bethlehem of Judea, in the days of King Herod, behold, magi from the east arrived in Jerusalem, saying, "Where is the newborn king of the Jews? We saw his star at its rising and have come to do him homage." When King Herod heard this, he was greatly troubled, and all Jerusalem with him. Assembling all the chief priests and the scribes of the people, he inquired of them where the Messiah was to be born. They said to him, "In Bethlehem of Judea, for thus it has been written through the prophet:

> 'And you, Bethlehem, land of Judah,
>   are by no means least among the
>   rulers of Judah;
> since from you shall come a ruler,
>   who is to shepherd my people Israel.'"

Then Herod called the magi secretly and ascertained from them the time of the star's appearance. He sent them to Bethlehem and said, "Go and search diligently for the child. When you have found him, bring me word, that I too may go and do him homage." After their audience with the king they set out. And behold, the star that they had seen at its rising preceded them, until it came and stopped over the place where the child was. They were overjoyed at seeing the star, and on entering the house they saw the child with Mary his mother. They prostrated themselves and did him homage. Then they opened their treasures and offered him gifts of gold, frankincense, and myrrh. And having been warned in a dream not to return to Herod, they departed for their country by another way.

Then they opened their treasures and offered him

gifts of gold, frankincense, and myrrh.

Luke 2:7

God's word strikes the heart. What word or phrase touched your heart?

How do the magi show us the way to be disciples of Christ? Give at least two examples.

Use this space to sketch or doodle the symbol for the Scripture—STAR

What are some of your "treasures?" How can you give them to God?

In prayer, offer Jesus your "treasures." Write down what He says to you.

_____
_____
_____
_____
_____

Notes

Notes

Notes

Notes

Credits

Page 17: *Animals entering the Ark* (fresco), Luini, Aurelio (c.1530-93) / San Maurizio al Monastero Maggiore, Milan, Italy / Mondadori Portfolio/Archiv Magliani/Mauro Magliani & Barbara Piovan / Bridgeman Images

Page 19: Image by PublicDomainPictures from Pixabay

Page 21: Wikimedia Commons / Public Domain

Page 23: Pixabay.com / Public Domain

Page 25: *God's Promise to Abraham* (oil on canvas), Tissot, James Jacques Joseph (1836-1902) / Jewish Museum, New York, USA / Public Domain

Page 27: Pixabay.com / Public Domain

Page 29: *Abraham leading his son Isaac to sacrifice*, illustration from Old Testament, end of 19th century, engraving by Bequet, Delagrave edition, Paris / De Agostini Picture Library / A. Dagli Orti / Bridgeman Images

Wikimedia Commons / Public Domain

Page 33: Wikimedia Commons / Public Domain

Page 35: Image by PublicDomainPictures from Pixabay

Page 39: flickr.com / Public Domain

Page 41: *Moses before the Burning Bush*, Room of Heliodorus, Vatican Museum (photo) / Godong/UIG / Bridgeman Images

Page 45: *Gathering of the Manna* (oil on panel), Master of the Gathering of the Manna (fl.1460-75) / Musee de la Chartreuse, Douai, France / Bridgeman Images

Page 47: Image of Quail / pixabay.com / Public Domain

Page 51: vecteezy.com

Page 53: *The fall of Jericho, walls come tumbling down as a result of the trumpets blown by the Israelites after walking round the city walls seven times* / Photo © Tamsin Priest / Bridgeman Images

Page 57: *Ruth and Naomi -Bible*, Dixon, Arthur A. (1892-1927) / Lebrecht Authors / Bridgeman Images

Page 61: *Eli and Samuel. And he said, 'It is the lord. Let him do what seemeth him good.',* Hole, William Brassey (1846-1917) / Private Collection / © L and Learn / Bridgeman Images

Page 63: Pixabay.com / Public Domain

Page 65: *Samuel anointing David in the midst of his brethren*, Hole, William Brassey (1846-1917) / Private Collection / © Look and Learn / Bridgeman Images

Page 69: Wikimedia Commons / Public Domain

Page 73: Wikimediia Commons / Public Domain

Page 77: *Elijah carried up into Heaven* (colour litho), English School, (19th century) / Private Collection / © Look and Learn / Bridgeman Images

Page 88: Flickr.com / Public Domain

Page 89: *Mother of Life*, Nellie Edwards / Used with Permission

Page 91: needpix.com

Page 92: *The Virgin Annunciate*, Batoni, Pompeo Girolamo (1708-87) (after) / Private Collection / Photo © Bonhams, London, UK / Bridgeman Image

Page 93: *Annunciation* (tempera on panel), Angelico, Fra (Guido di Pietro) (c.1387-1455) / Gemaeldegalerie Alte Meister, Dresden, Germany / © Staatliche Kunstsammlungen Dresden / Bridgeman Images

Page 95: pixnio.com / public domain

Page 96: *The Holy Family with the Infant St. John* (oil on fir panel), Luini, Bernardino (c.1480-1532) (after) / Apsley House, The Wellington Museum, London, UK / © Historic England / Bridgeman Images

Page 97: *Dream of Saint Joseph*, 1886-1890, by Modesto Faustini (1839-1893), fresco, Chapel of Saint Joseph or Spanish chapel, Sanctuary of Holy House, Loreto, Marche, detail, Italy, 19th century / De Agostini Picture Library / Bardazzi / Bridgeman Images

Page 99: needpix.com / public domain

Page 100: *No room at the inn*, illustration from 'Harold Copping Pictures: The Crown Series', c.1920's (colour litho), Copping, Harold (1863-1932) / Pri Collection / Bridgeman Images

Page 101: *Nativity* (tempera on wood), Bicci di Lorenzo, (1373-1452) / Chiesa di San Giovannino dei Cavalieri, Florence, Italy / Photo © Nicolò Orsi Battaglini / Bridgeman Images

Page 103: pixabay.com / public domain

Page 104: *Journey of the Magi*, c.1894 (oil on canvas), Tissot, James Jacques Joseph (1836-1902) / Minneapolis Institute of Arts, MN, USA / The Will Hood Dunwoody Fund / Bridgeman Images

Page 105: *Adoration of the Magi*, c.1405 (tempera on panel), Mariotto di Nardo, (fl.1394-1424) / Allen Memorial Art Museum, Oberlin College, Ohio, U / R.T. Miller, Jr. Fund / Bridgeman Images

Page 107: pixabay.com / public domain